Peanuts Lunchtime Cookbook

Charles M. Schulz

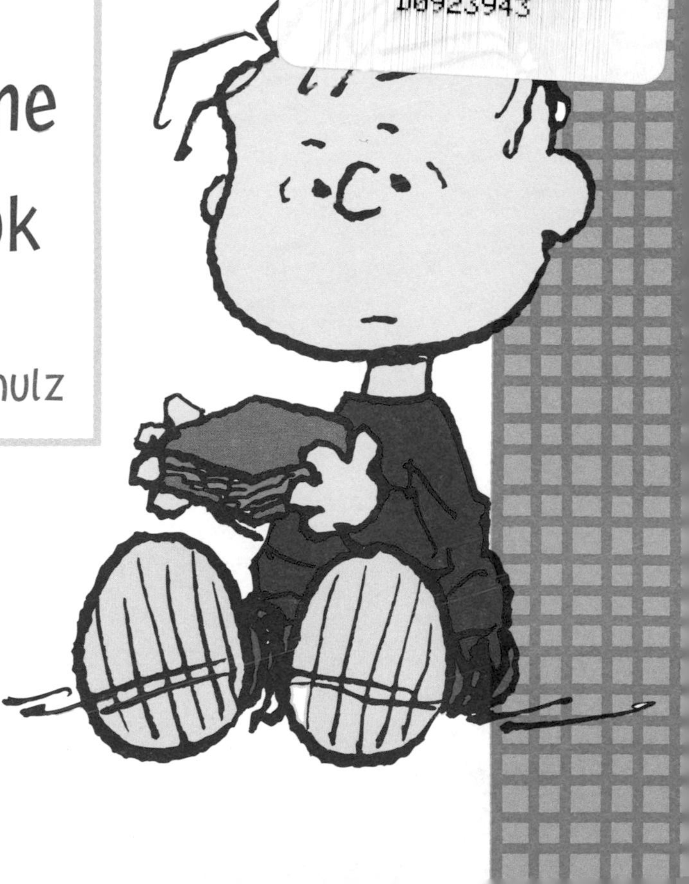

Ballantine Books
New York

A Ballantine Books Trade Paperback Original

Published in the United States by Ballantine Books, an imprint of The Random House Publishing Group, a division of Random House, Inc., New York.

BALLANTINE and colophon are registered trademarks of Random House, Inc.

The comic strips in this book were originally published in newspapers worldwide.

Grateful acknowledgment is made to the following for permission to reprint previously published and unpublished recipes:

Allrecipes.com: "Ants on a Log" submitted by Michelle O'Sullivan, "Banana Fritters" submitted by Julia Morris, "Basic Fruit Smoothie" submitted by Janelle, "Bean Quesadillas" submitted by Jennifer Oriss, "Easy Chili" submitted by Jean Bernola, "Easy Fruit Dip" submitted by Natalie L., "Easy Mac and Cheese" submitted by Zaina, "Easy Snack Wraps" submitted by Joan, "Grilled Peanut Butter and Jelly Sandwich" submitted by Chastity, "Spicy Pretzels" submitted by Valarie, and "Weiner Winks" submitted by Krista Tank. Copyright © 2005 by Allrecipes.com. Reprinted by permission of Allrecipes.com.

Clarkson Potter/Publishers, a division of Random House, Inc.: "Egg Salad Spread," "Sloppy Joes," "Mixed Potato Salad," and "Powerful Peanut Butter Sandwiches" from *The Pillsbury Complete Cookbook* by The Pillsbury Company, copyright © 2000 by The Pillsbury Company. Reprinted by permission of Clarkson Potter/Publishers, a division of Random House, Inc.

Jennifer Osborne: "Minibagel Pizzas," reprinted courtesy of Jennifer Osborne.

Jean Schulz: "Overnight Salad" and "Tuna Noodle Casserole," reprinted courtesy of Jean Schulz.

Library of Congress Cataloging-in-publication Data

Schulz, Charles M.
    Peanuts lunchtime cookbook/Charles M. Schulz.
        p. cm.
ISBN 0-345-47986-6
    1. Luncheons. I. Title. II. Title. II. Title: Peanuts lunchtime cookbook.

TX735.S38 2006
641.5'3—dc22   2006042794

Printed in the United States of America

www.ballantinebooks.com

9 8 7 6 5 4 3 2 1

Designed by Diane Hobbing of Snap-Haus Graphics

CONTENTS

READ THESE TIPS!

Before you begin making these Peanuts lunchtime favorites, here are a few things to remember:

1. Wash your hands before handling food.
2. Read the recipe all the way through and ask an adult about anything you don't understand. Then get out all the ingredients and equipment you will need.
3. Ask an adult for help if you will be using an electric mixer, blender, can opener, knife, or the oven.
4. When using a microwave oven, be careful as the contents may be very hot after heating.
5. Make sure you keep a tidy work area and clean any mess after you're done.
6. You can substitute some ingredients for low-calorie or low-fat versions (i.e. cheese, mayonnaise, etc).

Have fun and enjoy!

Egg Salad Spread

4 eggs
1 teaspoon chopped pimientos
1/2 teaspoon chopped chives
1/8 teaspoon salt
3 tablespoons mayonnaise or salad dressing
dash pepper

Place eggs in medium saucepan, cover with water, and bring to a boil. Reduce heat
and simmer about 15 minutes. Immediatly drain, and run cold water over the eggs to stop
cooking. Peel eggs and chop. In small bowl, combine eggs and all remaining ingredients.
Mix well and refrigerate.

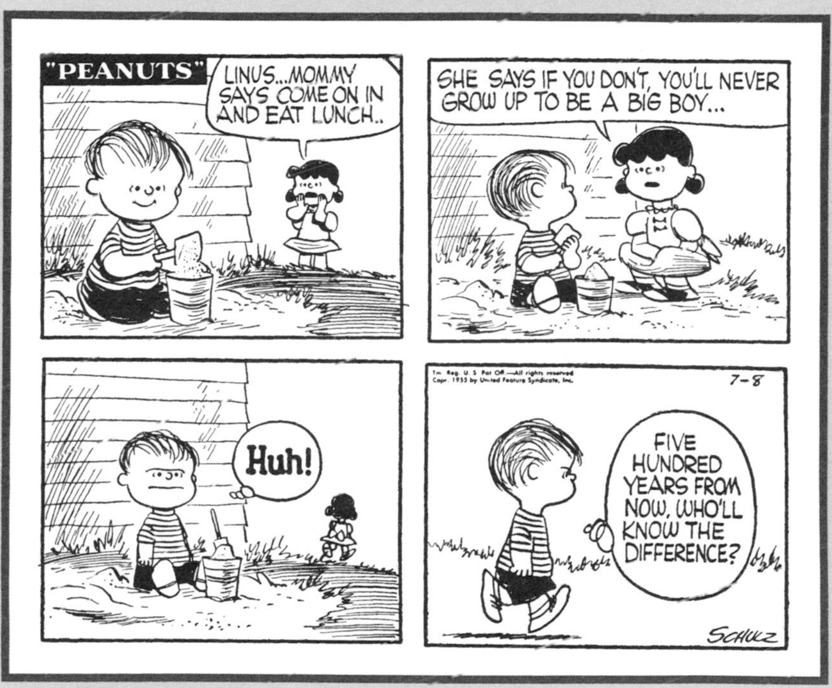
"PEANUTS"
LINUS...MOMMY SAYS COME ON IN AND EAT LUNCH..
SHE SAYS IF YOU DON'T, YOU'LL NEVER GROW UP TO BE A BIG BOY...
Huh!
Tm Reg. U. S. Pat Off.—All rights reserved
Copr. 1955 by United Feature Syndicate, Inc.
7-8
FIVE HUNDRED YEARS FROM NOW, WHO'LL KNOW THE DIFFERENCE?
SCHULZ

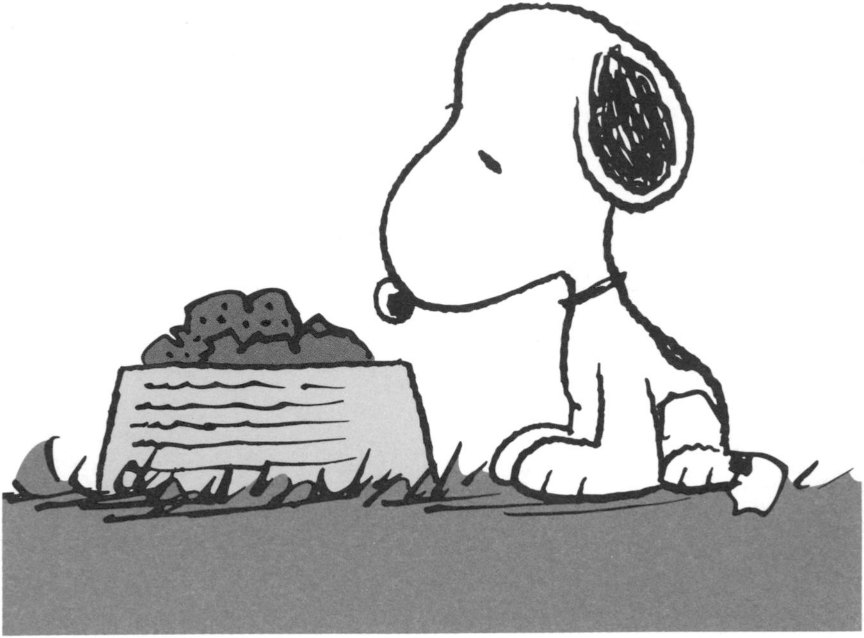

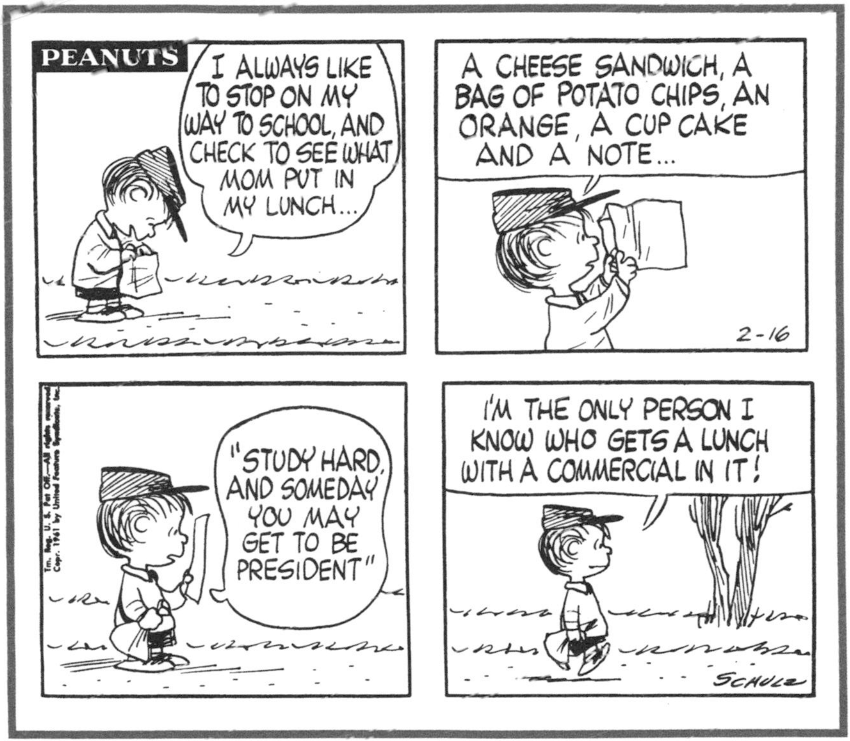
PEANUTS
I ALWAYS LIKE TO STOP ON MY WAY TO SCHOOL, AND CHECK TO SEE WHAT MOM PUT IN MY LUNCH...
A CHEESE SANDWICH, A BAG OF POTATO CHIPS, AN ORANGE, A CUP CAKE AND A NOTE...
2-16
"STUDY HARD, AND SOMEDAY YOU MAY GET TO BE PRESIDENT"
I'M THE ONLY PERSON I KNOW WHO GETS A LUNCH WITH A COMMERCIAL IN IT!
SCHULZ

Easy Fruit Dip

1 (8-ounce) package cream cheese, softened
1 (16-ounce) jar marshmallow cream
1 tablespoon maraschino cherry juice
fruit, pretzels, bread, for dipping

Place cream cheese and marshmallow cream in a microwave-safe bowl. Put the bowl in the microwave and cook on medium-high for 20-second increments, until softened.
Stir the maraschino cherry juice into the mixture. Cover and refrigerate until chilled.

Slice up a selection of fruit and snacks, like apples, strawberries, pretzels, and raisin bread, and serve with the dip.

PEANUTS
11-11
Tm. Reg. U S Pat Off.—All rights reserved
Copr. 1963 by United Feature Syndicate Inc.
I HATE LUNCH HOUR!
EVERY DAY I SIT HERE ON THIS BENCH ALL BY MYSELF EATING A PEANUT BUTTER SANDWICH...
SOME PSYCHIATRISTS SAY THAT PEOPLE WHO EAT PEANUT BUTTER SANDWICHES ARE LONELY.. ..I BELIEVE IT....
WHEN YOU'RE REAL LONELY, THE PEANUT BUTTER STICKS TO THE ROOF OF YOUR MOUTH...
SCHULZ

PEANUTS
I DIDN'T FEEL VERY WELL WHEN I GOT UP THIS MORNING..
MY MOTHER ALMOST KEPT ME HOME FROM SCHOOL..
FINALLY, SHE DECIDED I'D BETTER GO..
YOU LOOKED LIKE YOU WERE FEELING BETTER, HUH?
Tm. Reg. U. S. Pat. Off.—All rights reserved
Copr. 1964 by United Feature Syndicate, Inc.
4-3
NO, SHE HAD MY LUNCH ALL MADE!
SCHULZ

PEANUTS
DON'T TELL ME THAT'S YOUR LUNCH?!
SOME OF IT...
Tm. Reg. U. S. Pat. Off.—All rights reserved
© 1965 by United Feature Syndicate, Inc.
3-30
WHAT ELSE DO YOU HAVE IN THERE?
MY SKATE BOARD!
SCHULZ

Powerful Peanut Butter Sandwiches

Peanut Butter sandwiches with a twist!

1/4 **cup peanut butter**
1/4 **cup shredded carrot**
2 **tablespoons shelled sunflower seeds**
2 **tablespoons raisins**
2 **tablespoons honey or sugar**
4 **bagels, split, or 8 slices whole wheat bread**

In small container, combine all the ingredients, except the bagels, and mix well. Spread the mixture on 4 bagel halves or bread slices, and top with the remaining bagel halves or bread slices.

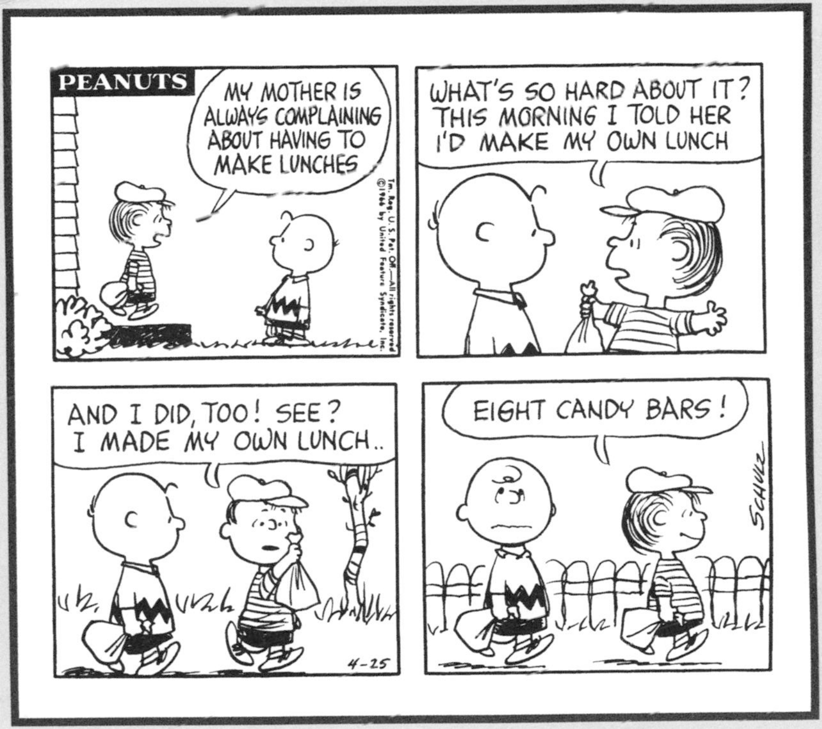
PEANUTS
MY MOTHER IS ALWAYS COMPLAINING ABOUT HAVING TO MAKE LUNCHES
Tm. Reg. U. S. Pat. Off.—All rights reserved ©1966 by United Feature Syndicate, Inc.
WHAT'S SO HARD ABOUT IT? THIS MORNING I TOLD HER I'D MAKE MY OWN LUNCH
AND I DID, TOO! SEE? I MADE MY OWN LUNCH..
4-25
EIGHT CANDY BARS!
SCHULZ

Grilled Peanut Butter and Jelly Sandwich

2 teaspoons butter
2 slices bread
1 teaspoon peanut butter
2 teaspoons any flavor fruit jelly

Heat a griddle or a skillet. Spread the butter on one side of each slice of bread. Spread the peanut butter on the unbuttered side of one slice of bread, and the jelly on the other. Place one slice, buttered side down, on the griddle. Top with other slice, so that the peanut butter and jelly are in the middle. Fry for 4 minutes on each side, or until golden brown and heated through.

PEANUTS
Tm. Reg. U. S. Pat. Off.—All rights reserved © 1968 by United Feature Syndicate, Inc.
I WISH OUR SCHOOL HAD A CAFETERIA..
IT WOULD GIVE ME A BETTER CHANCE TO MEET THAT LITTLE RED-HAIRED GIRL...
I'D SAY, "HELLO, LITTLE RED-HAIRED GIRL... MAY I TREAT YOU TO LUNCH TODAY?"
10-14
WHY NOT JUST ASK HER TO BROWN-BAG IT?
SCHULZ

Ants on a Log

5 stalks celery
$1/2$ cup peanut butter
$1/4$ cup raisins

Cut the celery stalks in half. Spread with peanut butter and sprinkle with raisins.

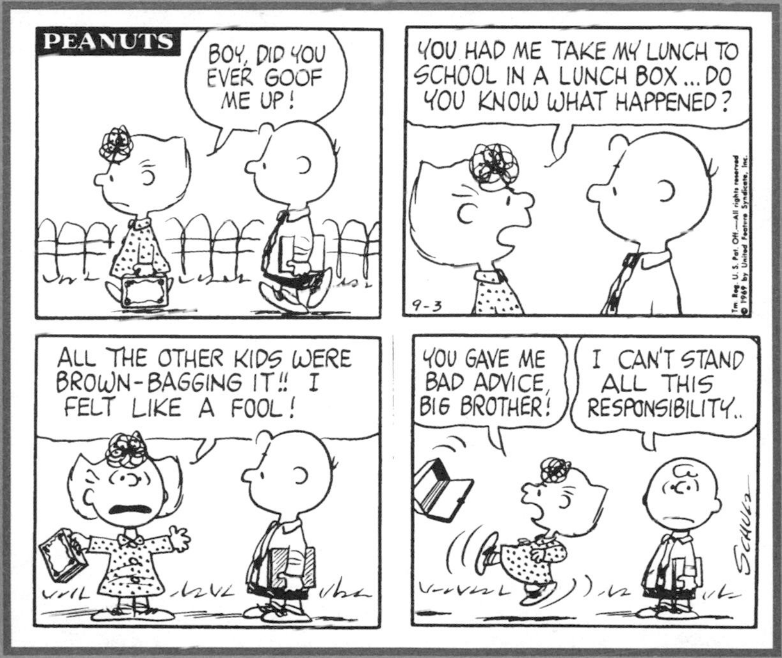
PEANUTS
BOY, DID YOU EVER GOOF ME UP!
YOU HAD ME TAKE MY LUNCH TO SCHOOL IN A LUNCH BOX ... DO YOU KNOW WHAT HAPPENED?
9-3
Tm. Reg. U. S. Pat. Off.—All rights reserved © 1969 by United Feature Syndicate, Inc.
ALL THE OTHER KIDS WERE BROWN-BAGGING IT!! I FELT LIKE A FOOL!
YOU GAVE ME BAD ADVICE, BIG BROTHER!
I CAN'T STAND ALL THIS RESPONSIBILITY..
SCHULZ

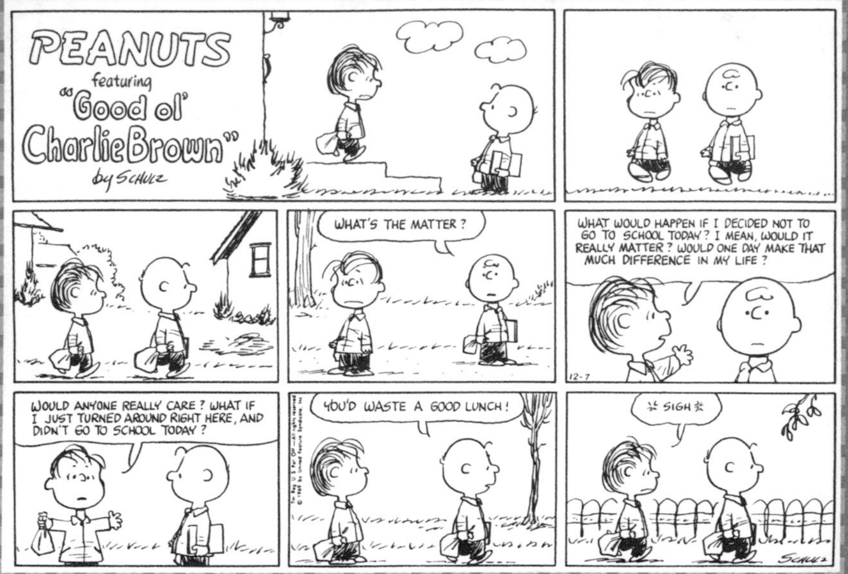
PEANUTS
featuring
"Good ol' CharlieBrown"
by SCHULZ
WHAT'S THE MATTER ?
WHAT WOULD HAPPEN IF I DECIDED NOT TO GO TO SCHOOL TODAY ? I MEAN, WOULD IT REALLY MATTER ? WOULD ONE DAY MAKE THAT MUCH DIFFERENCE IN MY LIFE ?
12-7
WOULD ANYONE REALLY CARE ? WHAT IF I JUST TURNED AROUND RIGHT HERE, AND DIDN'T GO TO SCHOOL TODAY ?
Tm Reg U S Pat Off—All rights reserved © 1969 by United Feature Syndicate, Inc
YOU'D WASTE A GOOD LUNCH !
SIGH
SCHULZ

PEANUTS
I'M STILL HUNGRY..
I ATE A PEANUT BUTTER SANDWICH, AN APPLE AND TWO COOKIES, BUT I'M STILL HUNGRY..
THAT ALWAYS USED TO BE ENOUGH FOR ME..
TRASH
Tm. Reg. U. S. Pat. Off.—All rights reserved © 1972 by United Feature Syndicate, Inc.
3-24
I THINK I'VE OUTGROWN MY LUNCH!
SCHULZ

Banana Fritters

Makes 2 dozen (approximately 6 servings)

A delicious sweet recipe that can be eaten for breakfast, too!

½ cup milk
2 bananas, mashed
2 cups all-purpose flour
½ teaspoon salt
3 teaspoons baking powder
2 eggs, beaten
1 tablespoon margarine, melted
1 quart vegetable oil for frying
½ cup confectioners' sugar

In a mixing bowl, combine the milk and the bananas. Sift in the flour, salt, and baking powder. Thoroughly mix in the eggs and margarine. Heat the oil in a large skillet. Carefully place spoonfuls of the mixture into the hot oil and fry until brown. Flip the fritters and continue to brown. Remove them from the oil and drain on paper towels. Dust the fritters with confectioners' sugar and serve while warm.

PEANUTS
YOU ONLY EAT THE CENTER OF YOUR BREAD?
1-19
THAT'S THE PART I LIKE
WHAT DO YOU DO WITH THE REST OF IT?
THROW IT TO THE BIRDS...
Tm. Reg. U.S. Pat. Off.—All rights reserved
© 1973 by United Feature Syndicate, Inc.
SCHULZ

PEANUTS
YOU HAVE TO GO TO SCHOOL, SIR...YOU CAN'T JUST QUIT!
WHY CAN'T I ? YESTERDAY ONE OF THE TEACHERS EVEN CRITICIZED MY LUNCH!
3-12
SHE SAID I HAD TOO MANY DOUGHNUTS AND NOT ENOUGH CARROTS...
IT'S TIME TO QUIT WHEN THEY EVEN CRITICIZE YOUR LUNCH!
SCHULZ

Easy Snack Wraps

Makes 60 servings (enough for a large party)

A great snack that takes only 15 minutes to prepare!

12 (10-inch) flour tortillas
1 (8-ounce) package cream cheese
1 head lettuce
1 (6-ounce) package sliced deli-style turkey
2 cups shredded carrots
2 cups minced tomatoes
toothpicks

Spread the cream cheese evenly over the tortillas. Top the cream cheese with lettuce leaves. Arrange the turkey slices in even layers on top of the lettuce. Sprinkle the carrots and tomatoes over the turkey slices. Roll the tortillas into wraps. Cut the wraps diagonally into bite-size pieces. Secure with toothpicks.

PEANUTS
I DREAD THE STARTING OF SCHOOL..
MY DAD SAYS I HAVEN'T BEEN EATING PROPERLY...
8-20
HE SAID HE'S GOING TO SIGN ME UP FOR A NEW COURSE...
BONEHEAD LUNCH!
SCHULZ

PEANUTS
WHEN YOUR LUNCH IS DULL, EVERYTHING IS DULL
5-8
HERE, CHARLIE BROWN... TRY ONE OF THESE..
WHAT IS IT?
Tm. Reg. U.S. Pat. Off.—All rights reserved © 1975 by United Feature Syndicate, Inc.
A PEANUT BUTTER DOUGHNUT!
SCHULZ

PEANUTS
Social Science Report
"What I learned in school this year."
Tm. Reg. U.S. Pat. Off.—All rights reserved
© 1973 by United Feature Syndicate, Inc.
5-27
This year I learned to keep an eye on my lunch so it doesn't get ripped off!
SCHULZ

Spicy Pretzels

a spicy shaken snack with bite!

1 teaspoon ground cayenne pepper
1 teaspoon lemon pepper
1 1/2 teaspoons garlic salt
1 (1-ounce) package dry ranch-style dressing mix
3/4 cup vegetable oil
1 1/2 (15-ounce) packages minipretzels

In a small bowl, mix together the cayenne pepper, lemon pepper, garlic salt, dressing mix, and vegetable oil. Place the pretzels in a large, sealable plastic bag. Pour in the mixture from the bowl. Shake well. Allow the pretzels to marinate approximately 2 hours before serving. Shake occasionally to maintain coating.

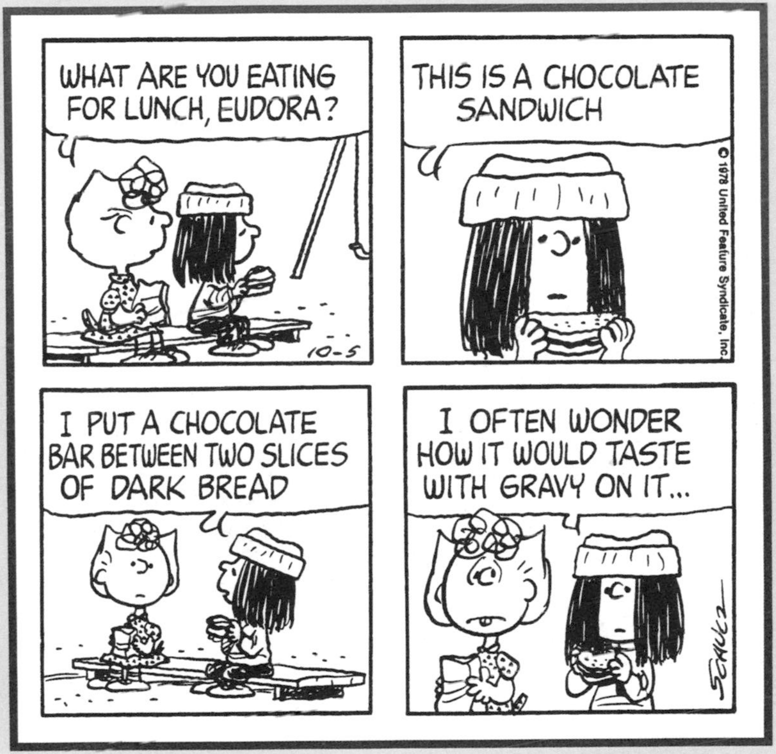
WHAT ARE YOU EATING FOR LUNCH, EUDORA?
10-5
THIS IS A CHOCOLATE SANDWICH
© 1978 United Feature Syndicate, Inc.
I PUT A CHOCOLATE BAR BETWEEN TWO SLICES OF DARK BREAD
I OFTEN WONDER HOW IT WOULD TASTE WITH GRAVY ON IT...
SCHULZ

HOW CAN YOU PIG-OUT ON ALL THAT JUNK FOOD EVERY DAY, SIR ?
© 1979 United Feature Syndicate, Inc.
LIFE IS MORE THAN CARROT STICKS, MARCIE
I'LL BET YOU'VE NEVER EVEN TRIED ONE, SIR
WHAT IS A STOMACH THAT'S EXPECTING A CHOCOLATE BAR GOING TO SAY WHEN IT GETS A CARROT STICK ?
5-2
EXPLAIN TO IT THAT YOU'RE ALL PART OF THE SAME TEAM, SIR..IT'LL APPRECIATE BEING INVOLVED...
SCHULZ

Weiner Winks

8 slices bread
8 teaspoons butter
8 slices processed American cheese
1 (16-ounce) package beef frankfurters
toothpicks

Preheat oven to 350° F. Take 1 slice of bread and spread 1 teaspoon of butter on one side. Turn the bread over and place a slice of cheese on the bread. Place a frankfurter diagonally on the cheese. Fold the bread corner to corner around the frankfurter. Insert a toothpick to hold it together and place it in a baking dish. Repeat with the remaining frankfurters. Bake for 20 to 30 minutes, or until golden brown.

MARSHMALLOWS? THAT'S YOUR LUNCH, SIR? A BAG OF MARSHMALLOWS?
I WAS IN A HURRY THIS MORNING, MARCIE, AND THAT'S ALL I COULD FIND IN THE KITCHEN...
5-26
WELL, I GUESS I HAD ONE OTHER CHOICE
WHAT WAS THAT, SIR?
ICE CUBES!
© 1980 United Feature Syndicate, Inc
SCHULZ

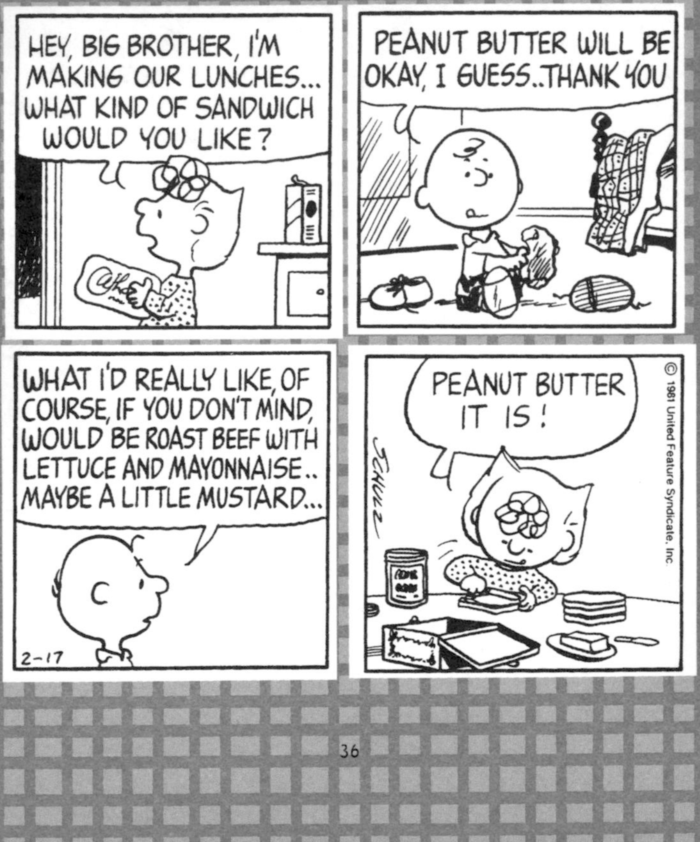
HEY, BIG BROTHER, I'M MAKING OUR LUNCHES... WHAT KIND OF SANDWICH WOULD YOU LIKE?
PEANUT BUTTER WILL BE OKAY, I GUESS..THANK YOU
WHAT I'D REALLY LIKE, OF COURSE, IF YOU DON'T MIND, WOULD BE ROAST BEEF WITH LETTUCE AND MAYONNAISE.. MAYBE A LITTLE MUSTARD...
2-17
PEANUT BUTTER IT IS!
SCHULZ
© 1981 United Feature Syndicate, Inc.

OKAY, BIG BROTHER, YOUR SANDWICH IS READY... BUT I DON'T KNOW HOW YOU'RE GOING TO CARRY IT...
YOUR LUNCH BOX IS BROKEN AND WE'RE ALL OUT OF PAPER BAGS...
DO YOU HAVE A PENCIL?
SURE, WHY?
© 1981 United Feature Syndicate, Inc.
2-18
SCHULZ

Bean Quesadillas

1 tablespoon plus $1/4$ cup vegetable oil
1 onion, finely diced
2 cloves garlic, minced
1 (15-ounce) can black beans, rinsed and drained
1 green bell pepper, chopped
2 tomatoes, chopped
$1/2$ (10-ounce) package frozen corn
12 (12-inch) flour tortillas
1 cup shredded cheddar cheese

Heat 1 tablespoon of oil in a skillet over medium heat, add the onion and garlic and sauté until soft. Mix in the beans, bell pepper, tomatoes, and corn, and cook until heated through. Spread 6 tortillas with equal amounts of the bean and vegetable mixture. Sprinkle with equal amounts of the cheddar cheese, and top with the remaining tortillas to form the quesadillas. Heat 1/4 cup of oil in a large skillet over medium-high heat. Place quesadillas one at a time in the skillet and fry, turning once, until cheese is melted and both sides are lightly browned.

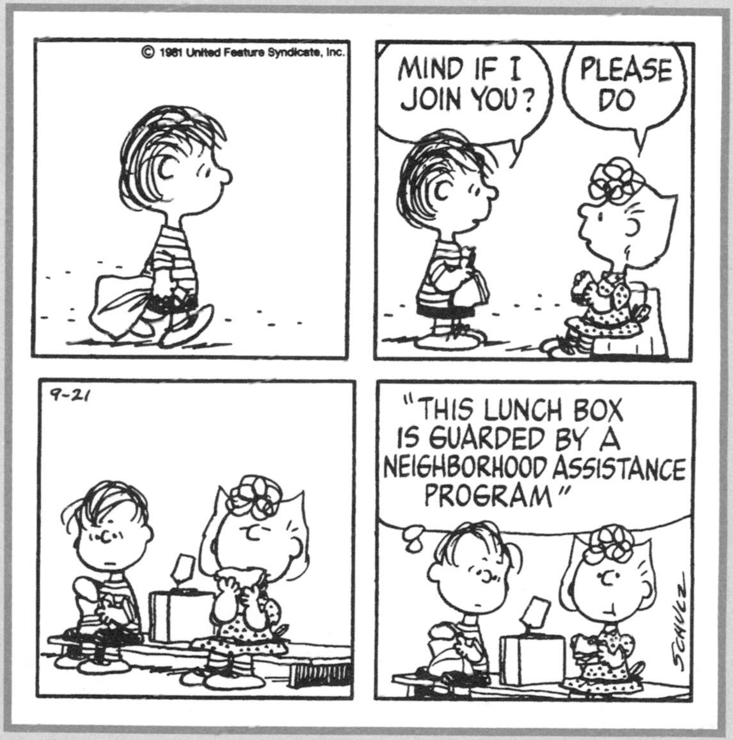
© 1981 United Feature Syndicate, Inc.
MIND IF I JOIN YOU?
PLEASE DO
9-21
"THIS LUNCH BOX IS GUARDED BY A NEIGHBORHOOD ASSISTANCE PROGRAM"
SCHULZ

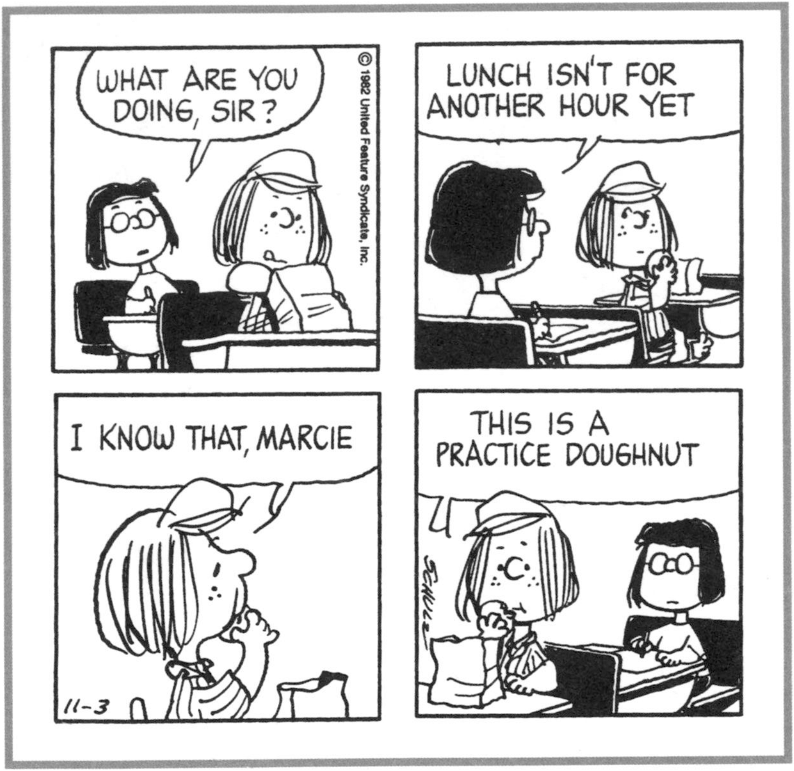
WHAT ARE YOU DOING, SIR?
© 1982 United Feature Syndicate, Inc.
LUNCH ISN'T FOR ANOTHER HOUR YET
I KNOW THAT, MARCIE
11-3
THIS IS A PRACTICE DOUGHNUT
SCHULZ

Easy Chili

1 pound ground beef
1 (16-ounce) can chili beans, drained
1 (14.5-ounce) can peeled and diced tomatoes with juice
1 small onion, chopped
$1/4$ cup chopped green bell pepper

In a medium saucepan over medium heat, cook the beef until brown. Stir in the beans, tomatoes, onion, and bell pepper; reduce heat and simmer for 30 minutes. Serve in your favorite bowl.

YOU'RE GOING TO BE PROUD OF ME, MARCIE
GUESS WHAT I HAVE IN MY LUNCH..AN APPLE!
9-18
WHERE IS IT? I KNOW I PUT IT IN HERE THIS MORNING...
© 1986 United Feature Syndicate, Inc
HERE IT IS..UNDERNEATH ALL THE DOUGHNUTS!
SCHULZ

Basic Fruit Smoothie

1 quart strawberries, hulled
1 banana, broken into chunks
2 peaches, pitted and sliced
1 cup orange-peach-mango juice
2 cups ice

In a blender, combine the strawberries, banana, and peaches. Blend until fruit is pureed. Add the juice and ice and blend some more until desired consistency. Pour into glasses and drink immediately, or fill up a thermos and take it with you!

...AND AN APPLE AND SOME CARROTS..
WHAT DO YOU HAVE?
A TUNA FLAT SANDWICH..
THE SCHOOL BUS RAN OVER MY LUNCH BOX!
© 1987 United Feature Syndicate, Inc.
10-19
SCHULZ

I BORROWED YOUR LUNCH BOX THIS MORNING, BIG BROTHER...
IT FELL OFF THE CURB, AND THE SCHOOL BUS RAN OVER IT..
10-20
MY LUNCH BOX! IT'S RUINED!!
MAYBE YOU COULD HAVE PANCAKES EVERY DAY..
SCHULZ
© 1987 United Feature Syndicate, Inc.

Sloppy Joes

a Pig Pen favorite!

1 pound lean ground beef
$1/2$ cup chopped green bell pepper or celery
$1/2$ cup chopped onion
1 tablespoon brown sugar
1 teaspoon dry mustard
$1/4$ teaspoon salt
$1/8$ teaspoon pepper
$1/2$ cup ketchup
1 tablespoon vinegar
1 tablespoon Worcestershire sauce
1 (8-ounce) can tomato sauce
6 sandwich buns, split

In large skillet, combine ground beef, bell pepper, and onion, and cook over medium heat for 8 to 10 minutes or until beef is thoroughly cooked, stirring frequently. Drain well. Add all the remaining ingredients except buns, and mix well. Cover and simmer 15 to 20 minutes, stirring occasionally. Serve in buns.

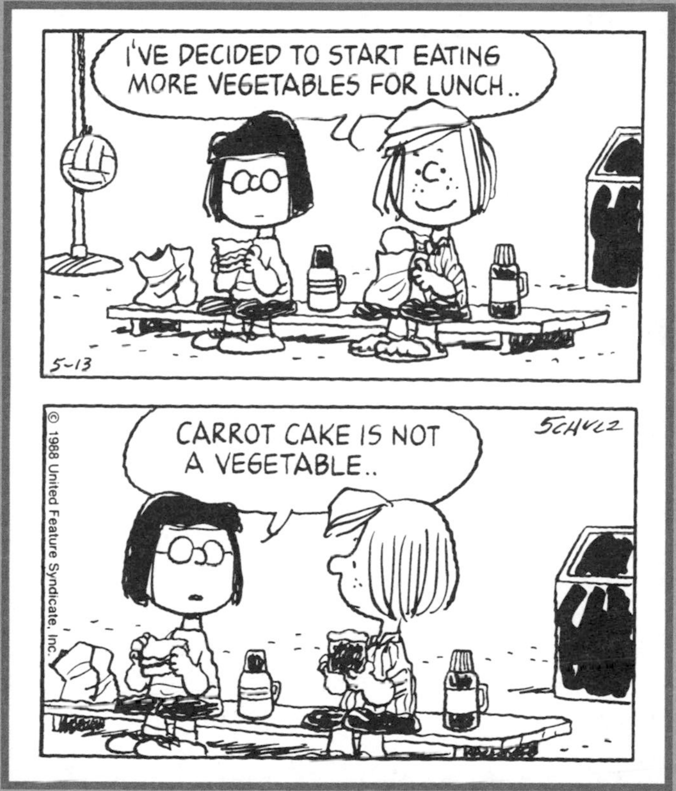
I'VE DECIDED TO START EATING MORE VEGETABLES FOR LUNCH..
5-13
© 1988 United Feature Syndicate, Inc.
SCHULZ
CARROT CAKE IS NOT A VEGETABLE..

Mixed Potato Salad

3 pounds red potatoes
2 pounds sweet potatoes
1 cup chopped celery
1 medium cucumber, peeled, seeded, and chopped

Dressing ingredients
1 (8-ounce) container nonfat plain yogurt
$1/4$ cup chopped fresh dill, or 1 tablespoon dried dill weed
$1/4$ cup light mayonnaise, or salad dressing
1 tablespoon lemon juice
$1/4$ teaspoon salt

Place whole red and sweet potatoes separately in 2 dutch ovens or large saucepans. Cover with water and bring to a boil. Reduce heat, and simmer until tender. Simmer red potatoes, 20 to 25 minutes; simmer sweet potatoes, 30 to 35 minutes. Drain potatoes and rinse with cold water to cool. Peel potatoes and cut into cubes. Place in large serving bowl. Add the celery and cucumber and mix well.

In medium bowl, combine all the dressing ingredients and blend well. Pour dressing over the salad and toss gently. Serve immediately, or cover and refrigerate until serving time.

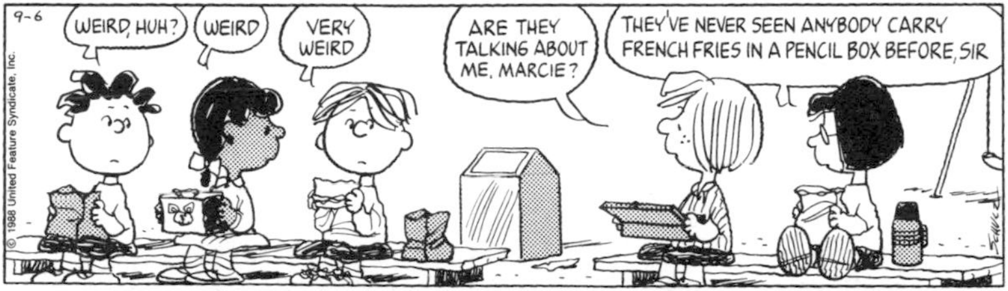
9-6
WEIRD, HUH?
WEIRD
VERY WEIRD
ARE THEY TALKING ABOUT ME, MARCIE?
THEY'VE NEVER SEEN ANYBODY CARRY FRENCH FRIES IN A PENCIL BOX BEFORE, SIR
© 1988 United Feature Syndicate, Inc.

PEANUTS
by SCHULZ
LUNCH
FOUR, THREE, TWO, ONE..
LUNCH TIME, MARCIE..
IS THAT ALL YOU'RE HAVING, SIR?. JUST FRENCH FRIES?
SO WHAT DO YOU HAVE THAT'S SO GREAT?
I HAVE A VERY HEALTHY LUNCH.. A CHEESE SANDWICH WITH SPROUTS, SOME CARROT STICKS, AN APPLE AND SOME CRANBERRY JUICE...
© 1989 United Feature Syndicate, Inc.
2-12
YOUR LUNCH SOUNDS HEALTHY ALL RIGHT, MARCIE, BUT IT ISN'T PERSONALIZED..
PERSONALIZED?
EACH FRENCH FRY HAS MY INITIALS ON IT!
SCHULZ

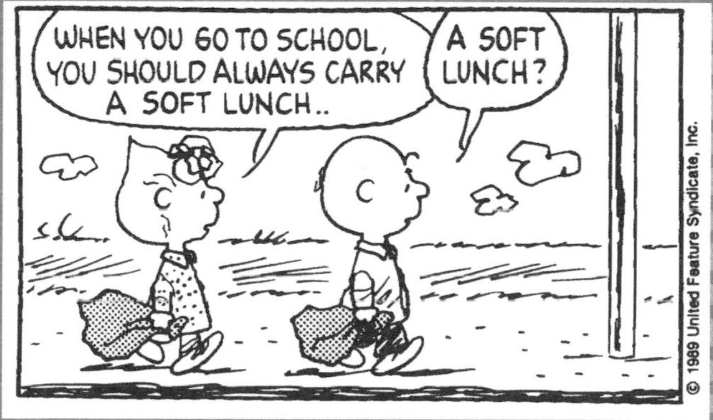
WHEN YOU GO TO SCHOOL, YOU SHOULD ALWAYS CARRY A SOFT LUNCH..
A SOFT LUNCH?
© 1989 United Feature Syndicate, Inc.

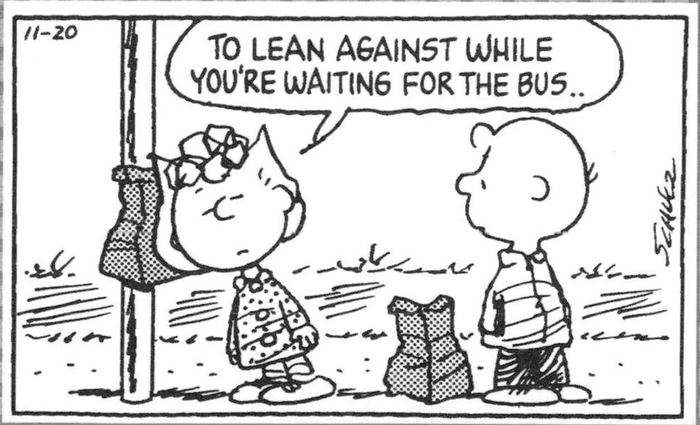
11-20
TO LEAN AGAINST WHILE YOU'RE WAITING FOR THE BUS..
SCHULZ

Easy Mac and Cheese

Makes 4 servings

1 cup macaroni
$1/2$ cup processed cheese sauce
2 frankfurters, sliced
1 teaspoon grated parmesan cheese
1 pinch dried oregano
4 buttery round crackers, crushed

Preheat oven to 350° F. Bring a large pot of lightly salted water to a boil. Add pasta and cook for 8 to 10 minutes or until al dente; drain. Heat the cheese sauce in a microwave for about 1 minute. In an 8-by-8-inch baking dish, combine the cooked pasta, cheese sauce, sliced frankfurters, parmesan cheese, and oregano. Top with crumbled crackers and bake for 10 minutes.

..AND A LITTLE MUSTARD, PLEASE.. THANK YOU...
I THINK I'LL HAVE THE "PLOUGHMAN'S LUNCH"
© 1990 United Feature Syndicate, Inc.
A HUNK OF BREAD, A SLAB OF CHEESE, A PICKLED ONION, A TOMATO AND A LETTUCE LEAF...
7-20
SO WHAT DO I GET? A HOT DOG!
SCHULZ

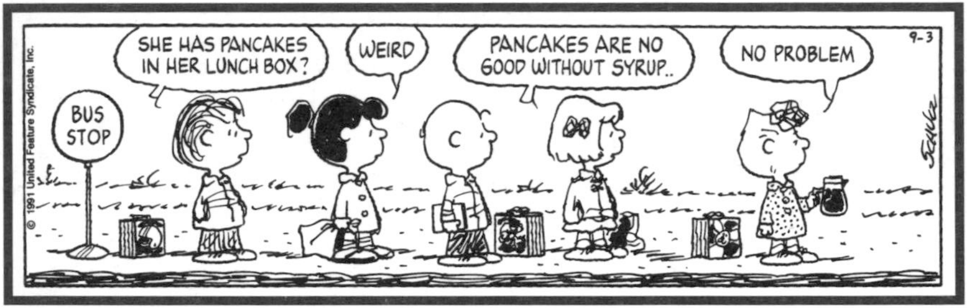
BUS STOP
SHE HAS PANCAKES IN HER LUNCH BOX?
WEIRD
PANCAKES ARE NO GOOD WITHOUT SYRUP..
NO PROBLEM
9-3
© 1991 United Feature Syndicate, Inc.

Minibagel Pizzas

6 minibagels, sliced
1 cup tomato sauce
1 cup shredded mozzarella
dry oregano
dry basil
salt to taste

Preheat oven to 350° F. Place 12 bagel halves on a cookie sheet. Spoon the tomato sauce on top of each. Sprinkle the oregano, basil, and cheese on each bagel piece. Bake for 20 minutes, or until the cheese is melted. Salt to taste and serve.

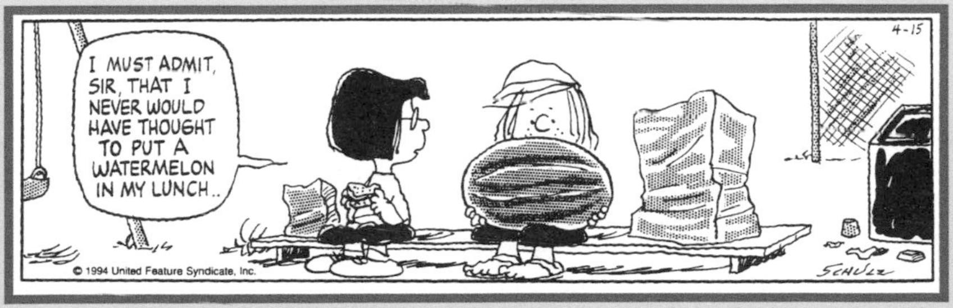
I MUST ADMIT, SIR, THAT I NEVER WOULD HAVE THOUGHT TO PUT A WATERMELON IN MY LUNCH..
4-15
© 1994 United Feature Syndicate, Inc.
SCHULZ

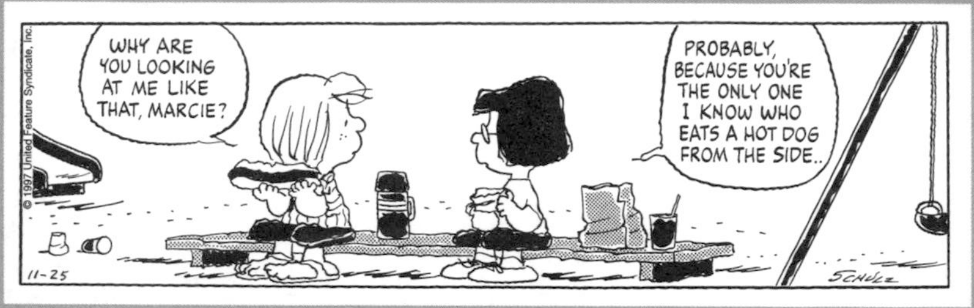
WHY ARE YOU LOOKING AT ME LIKE THAT, MARCIE?
PROBABLY, BECAUSE YOU'RE THE ONLY ONE I KNOW WHO EATS A HOT DOG FROM THE SIDE..
© 1997 United Feature Syndicate, Inc.
11-25
SCHULZ

Overnight Salad

This, and the Tuna Noodle Casserole, are Charles Schulz's favorite recipes!

$^1/_2$ **bag fresh spinach, stems removed**
$^1/_2$ **pound bacon, cooked and crumbled**
4 to 6 hard-boiled eggs
1 (10-ounce) package frozen peas, thawed
$^1/_3$ **head lettuce, chopped**
salt and pepper to taste
$^1/_2$ **tsp sugar**
$^1/_2$ **pound swiss or cheddar cheese, grated**
$^3/_4$ **cup mayonnaise**

Layer all the ingredients except the cheese and the mayonnaise. Between each layer, add salt and pepper to taste and sprinkle some of the sugar. Put the grated cheese on top and then cover with the mayonnaise. Refrigerate overnight. Toss before serving.

Tuna Noodle Casserole

2 cans tuna fish, drained
1 can condensed cream of mushroom soup (or any cream-based soup)
3 cups cooked egg noodles
1 (10-ounce) package frozen peas or broccoli
1 cup crushed potato chips or crispy fried onion rings

Preheat oven to 350° F. In a buttered 1½-quart casserole, mix together the tuna, soup, noodles, and vegetables. Sprinkle the top with the chips or onion rings. Bake for 20
minutes, or until heated through.

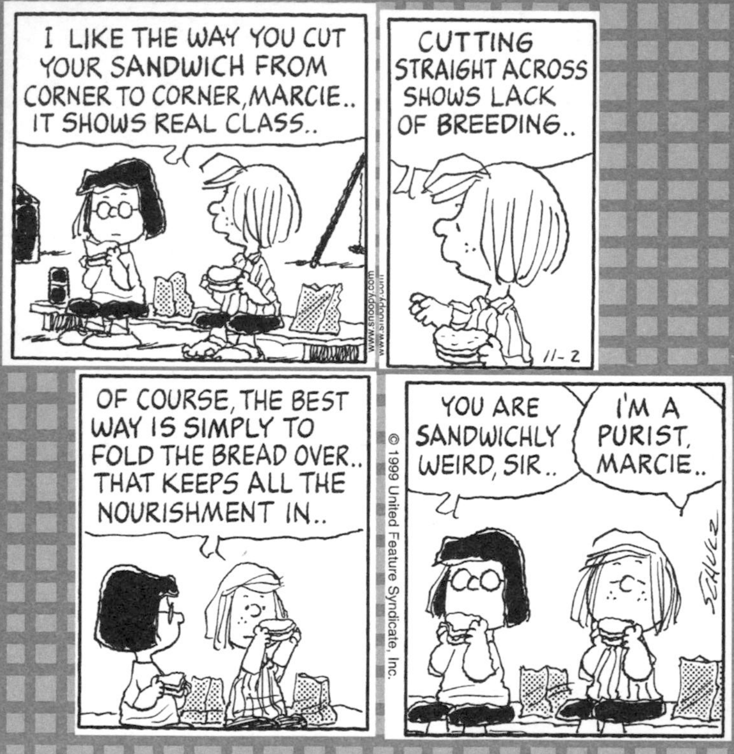
I LIKE THE WAY YOU CUT YOUR SANDWICH FROM CORNER TO CORNER, MARCIE.. IT SHOWS REAL CLASS..
www.snoopy.com
CUTTING STRAIGHT ACROSS SHOWS LACK OF BREEDING..
11-2
OF COURSE, THE BEST WAY IS SIMPLY TO FOLD THE BREAD OVER.. THAT KEEPS ALL THE NOURISHMENT IN..
© 1999 United Feature Syndicate, Inc.
YOU ARE SANDWICHLY WEIRD, SIR..
I'M A PURIST, MARCIE..
SCHULZ